DATE DUE

513
WAL

Walsh, Kieran
Music math

C. 1

$20.95
BC#34880000074125

DATE DUE	BORROWER'S NAME
1207	Diana. C.
3/25/08	

MUSIC MATH

Math and My World

Kieran Walsh

Rourke
Publishing LLC
Vero Beach, Florida 32964

www.rourkepublishing.com

PHOTO CREDITS:
All photos from AbleStock.com, except for page 24 by the author

Editor: Frank Sloan

Library of Congress Cataloging-in-Publication Data

Walsh, Kieran.
  Music math / Kieran Walsh.
     p. cm. -- (Math and my world II)
  Includes bibliographical references and index.
   ISBN 1-59515-493-0 (hardcover)
  1. Arithmetic--Juvenile literature. I. Title II. Series: Walsh, Kieran.
Math and my world II.

  QA115.W2684 2006
  513--dc22

                                    2005014990

Printed in the USA

w/w

TABLE OF CONTENTS

INTRODUCTION

Mathematics and music. Can you think of any ways that they might relate?

Maybe if you are taking lessons on an instrument you thought of different notes. Each key on a piano, for instance, creates a sound that is mathematically related to every other key on the piano.

Or, maybe you thought about buying music.

Can you read music? In some ways, it is like a mathematical equation.

CDs cost a lot of money, and if you have a large collection you can use math to figure out how much money you have spent in the past and how much you can afford to spend in the future.

In this book we will consider mathematics in relation to creating music and also in relation to enjoying music. You'll even use math to figure out how much music you can store on an MP3 player. The thing is, mathematics and music aren't just related, they are really the same thing. Music is the sound of math!

ENSEMBLES

Quick—who's your favorite musical artist?

Maybe you thought of a single person, or maybe you thought of a band made up of four or five people. You may even have thought of a symphony orchestra, which involves the talents and skills of many more people.

There are names for these kinds of musical groups. The most basic is the solo artist. A solo artist, of course, is just one person. That makes sense, since solo is a word meaning music for a single voice or **instrument**.

Solo = 1

After the solo artist, there are larger groupings of musicians. These groupings are sometimes called **ensembles**. What would be the next highest grouping after a solo artist?

One musician playing on his or her own is called solo.

The next step up is a duet. This is as simple as 1 plus 1:

$$1 + 1 = 2$$
$$\text{Duet} = 2$$

A group of three people, meanwhile, is called a trio:

$$\text{Trio} = 3$$

A group of four people is known as a quartet:

$$\text{Quartet} = 4$$

How many more people are there in a quartet than a duet?

$$4 - 2 = 2$$

There are two more people in a quartet than a duet!

Here are some more ensemble names:

$$\text{Quintet} = 5$$
$$\text{Sextet} = 6$$
$$\text{Septet} = 7$$
$$\text{Octet} = 8$$

How many more people are there in a septet compared to a quartet?

$$7 - 4 = 3$$

There are 3 more people in a septet than a quartet!

Let's compare an octet to a duet. One thing you can do is to subtract the smaller number from the larger number:

$$8 - 2 = 6$$

Now you can say that there are 6 more people in an octet compared to a duet. Another possibility, though, is to divide the larger number by the smaller number:

$$8 \div 2 = 4$$

Now you can also say that there are *4 times* as many people in an octet than there are in a duet!

It takes more people to form an octet than a duet. It takes many, many more people to form an entire orchestra.

Orchestras are ensembles that employ dozens of people. If there are 87 musicians in this orchestra, how many more musicians is that than in a trio?

This is because so many people are needed to play all the different instruments: trombones, violins, flutes, timpani…

The Ottawa Symphony Orchestra in Canada, for example, is made up of about 100 musicians. How many more musicians are there in the Ottawa Symphony Orchestra than in, say, a sextet?

$$100 - 6 = 94$$

The Ottawa Symphony Orchestra has 94 more musicians than there are in a sextet!

Not all ensembles are stationary! This marching band uses a number of musicians that play and walk at the same time.

The Biggest Orchestra

One hundred musicians may sound like a lot. The biggest orchestra ever assembled, though, was made up of 6,542 musicians! This massive ensemble performed at BC Place Stadium in Vancouver, Canada, on May 15, 2000.

How many more musicians were in that orchestra compared to the Ottawa Symphony Orchestra?

$$6,542 - 100 = 6,442$$

The largest orchestra ever had 6,442 more members than the Ottawa Symphony Orchestra. That's a lot of people making music!

NOTES AND OCTAVES

A very simple definition of music is that it is the combination of **rhythm** and **melody**. Rhythm is the pattern of music through time. Beats per minute is part of how rhythm is measured.

The rhythm for a piece of music is often kept by a percussion instrument like the drums.

But what about melody? Melody is a series of musical notes that follow a rhythm. Melody is what you hum to yourself while waiting for the school bus in the morning.

Different cultures have produced different styles of music. Most of what we are familiar with in the United States is called "western" music. It is called that because America is situated in the western **hemisphere**.

Much of western music is built using different combinations of just 12 tones, which are grouped into **octaves.** Some pianos may have more octaves than others, but no matter how long a **keyboard** is, it is always grouped into octaves.

The 12 notes in an octave are:

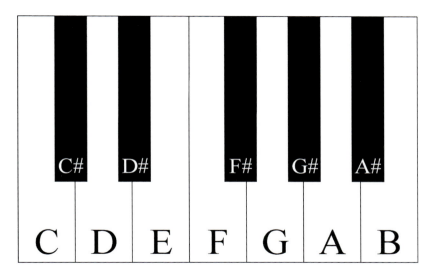

A standard piano usually has 88 keys. If there are 12 notes in an octave, how many octaves are there on a keyboard with 88 keys?

You can find out by using division:

$$88 \div 12 = 7.33$$

An 88-key keyboard contains about 7 octaves. You have to say "about," because there are a few extra keys. To be more specific, on a keyboard with 88 keys there are 52 white keys and 36 black keys.

How many more white keys are there than black keys?

$$52 - 36 = 16$$

There are 16 more white keys than black keys!

For the moment, we're going to focus on the white keys of a keyboard. Here are the 7 white notes:

C   D   E   F   G   A   B

On any keyboard, the "C" key that is closest to the middle of the keyboard is called "middle C."

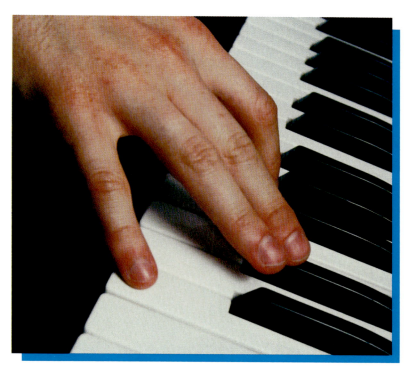

Middle C is just what it sounds like—the C note closest to the middle of a piano keyboard.

Even though you can't see it, sound is a **wave**. It travels through the air in much the same way that water ripples if you throw a stone into a pond. If you could look at a sound wave from the side, you would see that it resembles a mountain. It has a peak and a valley.

The journey from one valley up to the top of the mountain and back down again into the next valley is called a **cycle**. This is how sound waves are measured—in cycles per second. Another expression for this is *Hertz*, which is sometimes shortened to Hz.

The **frequency** of middle C on a piano is about 262 Hz. Here are the rest of the white note frequencies in the octave beginning with middle C:

D – 294 Hz

E – 330 Hz

F – 349 Hz

G – 391 Hz

A – 440 Hz

B – 494 Hz

What is the difference in the frequencies of A and C?

440 – 262 = 178 Hz

There is a difference of 178 Hz between A and C.

What about the difference between the frequencies of B and E?

494 – 330 = 164 Hz

Now we'll look at the black keys in this octave. Black keys are sometimes called sharps. Sharps are standard notes raised by a semitone, or half a tone. Here is a listing of the sharps in an octave. The "#" is a symbol for "sharp":

C#   D#   F#   G#   A#

Believe it or not, it's very easy to find out the frequencies of these notes. Take C# for instance. The frequency for C# is between the frequencies of C and D:

C – 262 Hz

D – 294 Hz

To find out the frequency of C#, you're going to find the **average** of C and D. This will be a two-step process. First, add the numbers of C and D:

262 + 294 = 556

Next, divide the result by the number of **addends**. Addends are the numbers you added together. In this case, there were 2 addends:

556 ÷ 2 = 278

The frequency of C# is about 278 Hz!

Sound travels in invisible waves like the ones imagined here. Using this illustration, can you chart one wave cycle?

Now find out the frequency of G#:

G – 391 Hz

A – 440 Hz

391 + 440 = 830

830 ÷ 2 = 415

The frequency of G# is about 415 Hz!

The problems you have been solving are all based on the notes in the octave beginning with middle C. However, you must understand that not every C note on a keyboard has a frequency of 262 Hz. For every octave above middle C, the frequency of a note will be doubled. For the octaves below middle C, the frequency of a note will be halved.

For instance, the next C note above middle C vibrates at a frequency of twice the rate of middle C:

262 x 2 = 524

The next C note above middle C vibrates at about 524 Hz!

So, if the A note in the octave of middle C has a frequency of 440 Hz, what is the frequency of the A note in the next octave up?

440 x 2 = 880

The answer is 880 Hz!

Radio Stations

Another instance where Hz is used is with radio stations. Let's say that your favorite radio station is 87.5 FM. What does that mean?

A radio station is usually identified by the frequency of the signal it broadcasts. A radio station located at 87.5 on the FM band is actually broadcasting at 87.5 **megahertz**. A megahertz is equal to 1 million cycles per second.

How many million cycles per second is 87.5 FM broadcasting? You can find out by multiplying:

$$87.5 \times 1,000,000 = 87,500,000$$

87.5 FM broadcasts at 87,500,000 cycles per second!

This radio is set to 91.1 FM. How many megahertz is that from your favorite FM station?

BEATS PER MINUTE

The next time you listen to one of your favorite CDs, try to notice how you react to it. Maybe you could even watch yourself in a mirror. You might be surprised to find that the music you really enjoy makes you move. You do things like bob your head, bounce your legs, or maybe even snap your fingers.

What you are doing, without even realizing it, is keeping time with the music. You are synchronized with the beat!

All music has a **tempo**. Tempo is a word that refers to the speed at which a particular selection of music is played.

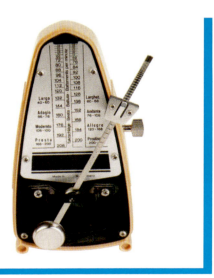

Pictured here is a metronome, a device used to set the tempo for a piece of music. Metronomes are especially useful for small groups of musicians who don't have a conductor to keep the time.

The reason why members of a symphony orchestra watch their conductor is because the conductor sets the tempo by waving his baton. Tempo is measured in terms of beats per minute, or bpm.

Most of the CDs you own and listen to have short gaps in between the songs. DJs, though, are supposed to keep everyone dancing. That is why disc jockeys play music in a similar fashion to how it is on the radio. Instead of spaces in between the songs, all the music is blended together. As one song fades out, the next begins. Really good DJs are even capable of **beat matching**. Beat matching provides a seamless flow of music. The records change, but to the average listener it all sounds like one long, continuous, stream.

Beat matching might sound easy, but it is a very difficult skill that takes years of practice to master. What makes beat matching so tricky is that almost every song has a different bpm count. That is why professional DJs keep notes of the bpm count for all the records in their collection. There are even books available for purchase on the Internet that list popular dance tracks and their bpm counts. Some companies manufacture devices that display the bpm count for a song while it plays.

Let's say that you are trying to match two recordings. The first recording, the one that is already playing, has a count of 142 bpm. The second recording, the one that you want to fade into the mix, has a count of 150 bpm.

What is the bpm difference between these two recordings?

You can find out by using subtraction. Just subtract the smaller number from the larger number:

$$150 - 142 = 8$$

Slowing down the second recording by 8 bpm should make it possible to match the 142 bpm count of the first recording!

Let's try another, more extreme example. What if you wanted to match two recordings with bpm counts of, respectively, 112 and 135? What is the difference in bpm between those?

$$135 - 112 = 23$$

The two recordings have a difference of 23 bpm!

Records are mostly out of fashion, but DJs still prefer them to CDs because they are easier to use when matching beats.

But how do DJs slow down, or speed up, a recording?

Most professional-level CD players have a pitch control that enables the DJ to alter the speed of a recording slightly. Different players vary, but a pitch control with a range of 8 percent is fairly common.

A percentage is a part of a whole. For instance, if a song has a tempo of 98 bpm, what would 50 percent of that be?

To find out, you first need to divide 50 by 100. This is because, literally, percent means a portion of 100:

$$50 \div 100 = 0.5$$

Next, you need to multiply the result, 0.5, by the tempo, 98 bpm:

$$98 \times 0.5 = 49$$

50 percent of 98 bpm is 49 bpm!

Club DJs keep the crowd on their feet and dancing!

As you've already learned, though, most of the CD players that DJs use only shift the speed of a recording by a tiny amount. So imagine that you have a recording with a tempo of 147 bpm. How much faster or slower can you make it with a pitch control of 8 percent?

First, divide 8 by 100:

$$8 \div 100 = .08$$

Now multiply the tempo by the result:

$$147 \times .08 = 11.76$$

Just for convenience, round this result up to 12.

Now you can say that, for a recording with a tempo of 147 bpm, you can alter the tempo by about 12 bpm. Remember, this means you can make it faster *or* slower by 12 bpm!

If this drum machine can keep a tempo of 320 bpm, how much faster is that compared to the average adult heartbeat?

Heartbeat

Even if you are not a musician, the idea of beats per minute should be familiar to you because it is also how we measure our heartbeat. The average heartbeat for an adult, for instance, is 72 bpm. If a piece of music has a tempo of 112 bpm, how much faster is that than the average adult heartbeat?

To find out, just subtract the smaller number from the larger number:

$$112 - 72 = 40$$

A tempo of 112 bpm is 40 bpm faster than the average adult heartbeat!

Try listening to your heart with a stethoscope. Does any of the music in your collection have about the same tempo as your heartbeat?

BUYING MUSIC

So far you've looked at different aspects of how music is created. The next step after that, though, is for someone to enjoy the music. This is where buying music comes into the picture.

CDs, or compact discs, have been around since the early 1980s. It is likely that they will continue to be the dominant form of music for some time to come.

You are probably familiar with two ways of buying music: CDs and downloading from the Internet. These methods are only the latest in a long line of systems for packaging and selling music, including records and tapes.

For this section, we're going to concentrate on the CD.

A standard CD can store approximately 74 minutes of music. Why 74 minutes became the standard CD length is unclear. Some stories about this assert that 74 minutes was chosen because that length of time would be able to hold an entire performance of Beethoven's Ninth Symphony!

If you know there are 60 minutes in one hour, can you find out how many hours of music a CD can hold?

$$74 - 60 = 14$$

A typical CD can hold about 1 hour and 14 minutes worth of music!

How many CDs do you own? Let's say, for example, you own 50 CDs. How many minutes of music is that?

$$74 \times 50 = 3700$$

50 CDs is equal to about 3,700 minutes worth of music!

You already know that there are 60 minutes in one hour, so how many hours is 3,700 minutes?

$$3700 \div 60 = 61.6$$

50 CDs hold about 62 hours worth of music. Since there are 24 hours in a day, how many days of music is that?

$$62 \div 24 = 2.58$$

50 CDs hold close to 3 days worth of music!

Now consider this: In the year 2004, people in the United States purchased about 666 *million* CDs! Written out, that number would be:

$$666,000,000$$

How many hours of music is that?

$$666,000,000 \times 60 = ?$$

You might feel a little intimidated because 666 million is such a large number. There is a trick you can use, though, to make finding the answer much easier.

First, remove all the zeros from the equation:

$$666 \times 6 = 3996$$

Now that you have a product, just tack on the zeros you removed to the end of that number. Remember to include the zero from 60, which makes the total number of zeros to add 7:

$$39960000000$$

And, once you add some commas, it starts to look like a manageable number again:

$$39{,}960{,}000{,}000$$

For convenience, you can round up that number and say that all the CD purchases in 2004 amount to about 40 *billion* hours worth of music! With numbers like that, you can see why the music industry is so profitable.

How much you pay for a CD depends on a lot of different factors: where you live, where you bought it, whether it was used or new, the popularity of the artist…

Imagine for a moment that you purchased all of the CDs in your collection at the same price—let's say $12. If you own 50 CDs, how much money have you spent on CDs?

$$50 \times 12 = 600$$

You've spent $600 on CDs!

◀ *Count the number of CDs in your collection. How many hours worth of music do you have? If you paid $12 each for them, how much have you spent on CDs?*

Now what about the total number of CDs purchased in the United States in 2004? If people bought 666 million CDs in 2004, how much money was spent on CDs? Use the same price—$12:

$$666,000,000 \times 12 = ?$$

Again, you can just remove the zeros to make calculations easier:

$$666 \times 12 = 7992$$

Now put the zeros back:

$$7,992,000,000$$

If you round the answer up, you can say that people spent about $8 billion on CDs in 2004! Now you can see why the music industry is so profitable!

The earliest records, 78s, were only capable of holding 4 minutes of music per side. How much music, total, did a 78 hold? ▶

<u>Records</u>

For a long time until the introduction of the CD, the dominant format for prerecorded music was the phonograph record.

The first records were called "78s." This was because they were recorded on discs that made 78 rotations per minute. Unfortunately, this meant only a small amount of music could be stored on each side of a 78—approximately 4 minutes.

In 1945, though, a new record format was introduced. This new format made 33 and 1/3 rotations per minute and was called the "LP," or long-playing record. The LP was capable of storing up to 25 minutes of music per side!

How much more music could one side of an LP hold compared to one side of a 78?

$$25 - 4 = 21$$

One side of an LP held about 21 minutes more music than one side of a 78!

MP3s

CDs have been with us since the early 1980s. And, while it is unlikely that they will disappear anytime soon, a more recent advance in technology has become a very popular new form of music. You are probably already familiar with it—MP3.

To understand how MP3s work, you have to go back to how sound works. Remember that sound is a wave. Earlier music technologies, like records and tapes, were systems that actually recorded copies of sound waves. These formats were known as **analog**.

CDs, like MP3s, are a digital music format, meaning that they translate music into a series of zeros and ones.

The CD, however, is a **digital** storage format. You may have noticed that part of that word is *digit*. Digit is really just a fancy word for number. That is precisely how CDs work. They store music as a series of numbers.

Digital recording is, in a way, like a series of pictures. Each of these pictures is a photograph of one little part of the sound wave that makes up the music being recorded. These pictures that are taken are called **samples**. The sample rate for a CD is 44,100 times per second.

So, if a song lasts 4 minutes, how many samples will that be?

First of all, you have to calculate how many seconds there are in 4 minutes:

$$4 \times 60 = 240$$

And then you have to multiply that result by the sample rate:

$$240 \times 44{,}100 = 10584000$$

A song that lasts 4 minutes will be made of 10,584,000 samples!

As you can see, in order for a CD to capture all the details of a sound wave, it needs to hold an awful lot of numbers. In fact, samples aren't even the end of the story. Each sample is further composed of smaller portions of information called bits. There are 16 bits for every sample.

If there are 44,100 samples per second, how many bits are there in a second?

$$44,100 \times 16 = 705,600$$

There are 705,600 bits in every second!

There is one more element to consider here, though. Most of the recorded music we listen to is in **stereo**. Basically, this is an attempt to mimic the way people hear with a left and a right ear. That is why a stereo recording is made of two channels, one meant for the left-hand speaker and one for the right-hand speaker.

If there are 705,600 bits in every second, and two channels are needed for stereo recording, how many bits are required for stereo recording?

$$705,600 \times 2 = 1,411,200$$

1,411,200 bits per second are needed for stereo recording!

But not all of those bits are needed to create a decent recording. In fact, many of them can be discarded without a person even noticing a change in the sound. This is the secret of MP3 technology.

MP3 is really a **compression** technology. It takes a large amount of data and compresses it into a smaller amount.

You may already have some knowledge of the terms used for digital storage. These include **megabyte**, **gigabyte**, and **terabyte**. The common factor in all those words is the term *byte*. **Byte** is simply a word for 8 bits.

A moment ago, you calculated that 1,411,200 bits per second are needed for stereo recording. Using division, can you calculate how many bytes that would equal?

$$1,411,200 \div 8 = 176,400$$

Stereo recording requires about 176,000 bytes per second!

If 176,000 bytes are needed for every second of a stereo recording, how many bytes are there in a 5-minute stereo recording?

First, you have to find out how many seconds there are in 5 minutes:

$$60 \times 5 = 300$$

Then you have to multiply that result by the number of bytes per second:

$$176,000 \times 300 = 52,920,000$$

MP3 technology has changed the way people think about their computers. Nowadays, they are seen as sophisticated home entertainment centers rather than just a business tool.

There are about 53 million bytes in a 5-minute stereo recording. This number can also be expressed in terms of megabytes. There are roughly 1 million bytes in one megabyte. Knowing that, how can you express a song that is composed of 53 million bytes in terms of megabytes?

$$53{,}000{,}000 \div 1{,}000{,}000 = 53$$

A 5-minute stereo recording will take up about 53 megabytes, or 53 MB!

53 MB is the amount of data needed to store a 5-minute stereo recording in an *uncompressed* format. Using MP3 technology, though, the amount of space needed for a 5-minute song can be shrunk considerably. In many cases, this can be done up to a **factor** of 10 or even 14.

Factors are very easy to understand. They are simply the numbers that create a product in a multiplication equation. For instance:

$$7 \times 12 = 84$$

In this equation, 7 and 12 are the factors, while 84 is the product.

So when we say that a 53 MB song can be shrunk by a factor of 10, what we're really saying is something like this:

$$? \times 10 = 53 \text{ MB}$$

The question mark in the equation above is the number of MB our 53 MB song can be shrunk to. How can you find that number? The easiest way is to move some of the numbers in the equation around and change it from a multiplication problem into a division problem:

$$? = 53 \div 10$$

5.3 MB!

Using MP3 technology, you can shrink an uncompressed song lasting 5 minutes to about 5 MB. How many megabytes less is that from the uncompressed recording?

$$53 - 5 = 48 \text{ MB}$$

That's 48 MB smaller!

If you're very lucky, you may own an MP3 player. These gadgets are used to store and play MP3 files. Most MP3 players include enough space to hold several hours of MP3 files. One of the smaller models holds about 10 gigabytes, or 10 GB, worth of music.

1 gigabyte is equal to about 1,000 megabytes. How many megabytes can a 10 GB MP3 player hold?

$$10 \times 1,000 = 10,000$$

A 10 GB MP3 player can hold about 10,000 MB!

So, let's say that you've converted most of your CD collection into MP3 files of about 5 MB in size. How many MP3 files of that size could a 10 GB player hold?

$$10,000 \div 5 = 2,000$$

A 10 GB MP3 player can hold about 2,000 songs!

Inside an MP3 player is a hard disk like this. If this hard disk can store up to 60 GB, how many songs can it hold?

Purchasing MP3s

There are a number of online music sites that will allow you to purchase MP3s for a very small cost. Typically, the prices run about $1 for every song.

What if you wanted to purchase and download an album with 16 tracks on it. How much altogether would that cost?

$$1 \times 16 = 16$$

Purchasing an album with 16 tracks would cost $16!

CONCLUSION

Maybe now that you've finished this book, you'll relax by listening to one of your favorite CDs. When you do, think about all the numbers that went into composing, recording, and buying that music. The fact is, music is all about numbers and math. You can't have one without the other.

So the next time you hear people (maybe even yourself!) say that math isn't any fun, just ask them how much they like music!

The next time you're at a concert, ask yourself: Is math fun?

GLOSSARY

addends — the numbers added together in an addition problem

analog — data in a continuous wave

average — a number used to represent a group of numbers

beat matching — combining two different works of music with similar tempos and beats

byte — a unit of digital memory; a group of 8 bits

compression — the method of reducing a large amount of data into a much smaller amount

cycle — in a wave, the distance from one point on the wave to the next corresponding point; from one valley to the next

digital — data broken down into small portions

ensembles — groups of musicians who perform together

factor — the amount by which a quantity is multiplied or divided

frequency — the number of wave cycles in a given period of time, usually seconds

gigabyte — one billion bytes

hemisphere — half of a sphere; part of the Earth as divided into north and south by the equator and east and west by the meridian

instrument — a device used to create music

keyboard — the set of keys on a piano

megabyte — one million bytes

megahertz — one million cycles per second

melody — an arrangement of musical notes

octaves — groups of 12 tones

rhythm — the pattern of music through time

samples — small parts of something bigger

stereo — sound in two channels; one channel for the left ear and another for the right ear

tempo — the speed of music; the measurement of beats per minute

terabyte — one trillion bytes

wave — an undulating form made up of peaks (crests) and valleys (troughs)

Further Reading

Slavin, Steve. *All the Math You'll Ever Need.* John Wiley and
Sons, Inc. 1999.

Zeman, Anne and Kate Kelly. *Everything You Need to Know
About Math Homework.* Scholastic, 1994.

Zeman, Anne and Kate Kelly. *Everything You Need to Know
About Science Homework*. Scholastic, 1994.

Websites to Visit

http://computer.howstuffworks.com/mp3.htm
How Stuff Works – How MP3 Files Work

http://www.learnpianoonline.com/
Learn Piano Online

http://www.discjockey101.com
Disc Jockey 101

INDEX

ABOUT THE AUTHOR

Kieran Walsh has written a variety of children's nonfiction books, primarily on historical and social studies topics, including the Rourke series *Holiday Celebrations* and *Countries in the News*. He lives in New York City.

3 4880 05000018 6
Koomen, Michele.

Size : many ways to
measure

$18.07

DATE DUE	BORROWER'S NAME	ROOM NO.
9-10-07	Rogelio H.	306
RIC	ard eCystro	
10-16-02	Aziah Bates	
11-20	Solanche	
11-21-07	Angel o	101
	Brandi	211
13-12	Tengi wilson	10
	Maleyi C-	215
	Ashley	
9/8/09	Valerie Lopez	215

DATE DUE	BORROWER'S NAME	ROOM NO.